T0162284

Swamp Candles

Winner of the Iowa Poetry Prize

Swamp Candles

POEMS BY RALPH BURNS

University of Iowa Press Ψ Iowa City

University of Iowa Press,

Iowa City 52242

Copyright © 1996 by Ralph Burns

All rights reserved

Printed in the United States

of America

Design by Richard Hendel

No part of this book may be

reproduced or used in any form

or by any means, electronic or

mechanical, including photo-

copying and recording, without

permission in writing from the

publisher. This is a work of poetry;

any resemblance to actual events or

persons is entirely coincidental.

Printed on acid-free paper

Library of Congress

Cataloging-in-Publication Data

Burns, Ralph, 1949 –

Swamp candles: poems / by Ralph Burns.

p.   cm. — (The Iowa poetry prize)

ISBN 0-87745-539-2 (pbk.)

I. Title.   II. Series.

PS3552.U732493S93   1996

811'.54—dc20   95-50367

CIP

01   00   99   98   97   96   P   5   4   3   2

For **Candace** *&* **William**

Contents

Acknowledgments

Some of these poems have appeared in these magazines, to which grateful acknowledgment is made: *Crazyhorse*, "Try"; *Field*, "Stella," "A Boat Is a Lever," and "Aunt"; *Gettysburg Review*, "Son, When I Hold You Tightly," "Memory," and "In the Bathroom Mirror"; *Graham House Review*, "The Happy Story" and "To My Father in Heaven"; *Indiana Review*, "Anniversary of Wood" and "Force"; *Ohio Review*, "Two Birds" and "The Man Who Patched the Floor"; and *TriQuarterly*, "First Flight" and "For My Wife, on Our Son's Third Birthday."

Thanks to the National Endowment for the Arts for a grant during the writing of some of these poems.

Stella

Stella

1

Flap, flap went the mind of the bird
who flew out of my grandmother's attic
like heat in the creases
where air used to be. One week
of summer was all that house
could take of my brother and me.

              Years later,
after she died, someone, my aunt I
think, arranged for her to be driven
back to Kingfisher, Oklahoma for the
funeral. It was raining, the mortician
hadn't arrived yet, so the driver
left her there—

my grandmother, unembalmed, in darkness,

in the month of the Green Corn Ceremony.
But she wasn't Cherokee, she hated Indians.
Her story was only deep, irregular
wing-beats of the heart.

Down dropped a huge bright-colored
night-bird with large crested head,
which, when raised, gave
the appearance of being startled.

It skimmed a few puddles gorging
on insects and a lizard or two.
Then banked south for my
grandmother's house, bright star.

2

Out out,
the bumblebee caught in the Pepsi
bottle, one of twelve
in the wood crate cooking
in the shed

and Arthur Van Horn drawing
bow and resin across
catgut, sour linen under
the fiddle, rosewood
cradled

under the chin—his new baby
cries her first cry
of a thousand,
for she is Stella,
after the guitar,

because rain and tears
are separate.

3

Those cuff links, that blowfish,
that stuff in the Hefty bag
are trash of my people—whose
bonds are movable like my

mobile grandmother idling
in the parking lot of La Quinta.
Whosoever speaks her name
fast in the window brings forth

light.

4

The ballpark all lit up
did not exist until we turned
her transistor on and some kid
whacked a rock back, back . . .

it knocked three feathers
off the mercury vapor, landed on corrugated
tin so that the interdigitated
interrupted their sleep but will

not be entering this poem.
They can just go back to pressing
on the chest like sorrow and letting
the game sink in its yellow

case with seventy-two holes
for the speaker and a carrying
strap. When the radio broke
I could not sling it like David

because the strap broke too.
But that was long after sound
commingling with a high brief whistle
amid chatter and crack of the bat.

You wouldn't have known her,
I can hear my cousin say.
Her hair was all gray.
It used to be red

but gray is something I heard
like the water-sucking clay.
But red is what she was
who like a star revolved

between three holes of light
or hung like an eye-droop
in water-cooled air and a dark
wind takes the summer.

5

There is the sound
	Brando makes under
		the wrought iron balcony

in New Orleans in summer
       and Stella sweats
             in her nightgown

and Desire runs
       along its length
             but all you hear

is Stanley—everybody
       knows—one word, two
             syllables, and even the space

between the stars is awestruck
       that a man can feel such
             stubborn, stupid language

crawl out of his brain,
       into his mouth, and scrape
             the ceiling of heaven—

Stella—you are beyond.
       Stella—knock, knock.
             I tap the limousine glass

like an ape, like Stanley
       Kowalski interdicting silence.
             Stella—the lights come on

in rooms 3 and 12, a hot
       humid air turns to pink smoke
             against the cool adobe wall.

A Boat Is a Lever

—after Simone Weil

After my student went to the doctor to
check out the rash speckling his
right hand and found out he had
leukemia, that the cancer had spread
into his lungs, then where did he go?
I've called his number several times.
Flat-bottom boats light in water.
Brown brack and mud smell,
stumps like chewed-off candles,
cypress knees, a knock and small
talk floating over water, a motor
chuffing off, a small blue cloud of excess
gasoline spreads an ugly
rainbow on tan water. Every
thing rests on its proposition
including smooth isobars along the bay.
*Since collective thought cannot exist
as thought it passes into things.*
Chemo takes a few gray hairs. Mustard
cruises the bloodstream under a blizzard
of white cells. Subdued by the arbitrary,
suspended, the one in the boat still needs
to row it—to direct the muscles, to
maintain equilibrium with air
and water. If water is waveless
then the boat reads by leading marks.
*There is nothing more beautiful
than a boat.*

Aunt

You don't have to do that, and as
she talked she tugged at her gloves.

Your uncle and I will keep you
and your brother for as long as you

want to stay. Don't have to do what?
Think what you're thinking. Her straw hat

shaded a planet. When we talk now
it's telephonic snow yoked by her

whisper from so many Kansas summers,
like corn silk under dust of chemo.

She almost finds her rhythm, that
of my mother, her sister. . . .

That must have been what. I was thinking
about her ninety pounds and the fact

that she would leave me, me intact,
not remembering, losing this moment

when grace enters a room with shears
with speckled mud and grass stem

and a voice with laughter ringing,
something you could see turned up

on one edge of its smile, light
and nothing else, self-compassion

and so, dialogue, all those years ago
without knowing. I could not have

(fresh from plucking okra in her white apron)
known the sweetness of the time.

I think I do now and I am wrong
again to refuse to think and listen

to her monotonous sadness, her refusal
to be other than she is . . . she is

sick and dying, almost dead,
wanting to be dead because living

one expects an active relationship
with death, preparation, not

understanding, that which is alone.
I think of her in afternoons when

she'd work a stiffness out by clipping
grass or pruning. A caterpillar

stretches and wrinkles on a volunteer
then steps off the frame, onto a Big

Boy leaf, then nods halfhearted extended
assent effacing a moment's breeze.

The Life Ever After

Two Birds

He leaving flew,
he flying left her there
    with nothing much to do
to keep from calling you, you,
    you, you. . . .

    Or so it seemed to me.
Until he dove and diving
    reached for her
with his feet, touched
    her lightly

    on the back that both
might touch talons, rolling over
    and over in the air.
I see their sulphur-colored bellies
    but I don't give

    a flying fuck for looking up above.
If they thought, they couldn't
    write it down,
that mating's not for life
    and traffic continues.

And if they thought
their figure eights and mile-long
    dives were pure projection
of what I see and hear with stiffness
    in my neck, I think

    they'd say I wasn't being candid.
But my warning's like theirs,
    having to do with territory.
I have sat with love on a tall wire.
    I think I must be crazy

    not to remember that life.
Or this one. I thought,
    so what, and didn't write
it down. But so what
    if I had. What absurdity

    to write it down.
That synapse leap of leaves
    in cold fall air.

The Man Who Patched the Floor

"A lot of people say they're baptized
like water's what saves you but
it's not. Fish swim in it,
people bathe in it. It's not water . . .
you can get baptized in it till the turtle
calls you by name . . . it's faith.

You're an educated man—you know
there's a sac around the heart. When Jesus
died they pierced that sac and water ran out.
He died of a broken heart. Not
many people know that."

*

He smelled like wood or varnish,
things you'd think of. His happiness
was too much, too little
to watch or listen to . . . and so
I walked away. But if I was bored
or put off by his direct stare and need
"to testify," why do I look where
the hole used to be, why remember
him at all—as a soul? I don't
even care what his name is, or that he
confounded oak with phony maple stain.
Surely what I want is life ever after,
not the that's that of a good story.
No wonder he left his chisel and drove

away in a Lincoln with gold lettering
on the back like the embossed spine of a Bible
I threw in the river long long ago.
By then I'd married young and divorced,
I'd been baptized ten maybe fifteen times.
I'd taken the crooked path
up the basement, past a street called
Central. I'd slept somewhere for free
though they made me pray for supper.
And from that sleep I'd listened
through a wall going orange then
blue to something like a moan.
I didn't know it but those sounds
had history. Their water trickled,
softly and tenderly, tenderly
calling their names like turtle doves
who sicken in the hot urban shade.

In the Bathroom Mirror

He continues to ponder
    and his wife moves next to him.
She looks. They look at themselves
    looking through the fog.
She has a meeting she says in about
    thirty minutes, he has
something too. But still she has
    just stepped out of the bath
and a single drop of water
    has curved along her breast
down her abdomen and vialed in
    her navel then disappeared
in crimson. Unless they love
    then wake in love
who can they ever be? Their faces bloom,
    a rain mists down, the bare
bulb softens above the glass,
    so little light that
the hands mumble deliciously,
    that the mouth opens
mothlike, like petals finding
    themselves awake again
at four o'clock mid shade and sun.

First Flight

I shucked my lucky clothes and jumped in,
swam beyond the bushes, thick canebrake
until I reached a tangle of grapevine and low
mesquite which hid me from the party. I listened.
I think that's when I saw her breast. . . .
I saw him kiss her breast.
I leaned on a hinge of small mesquite.
A sound unearthed itself from his throat. *Hey boy,
is that you?* I scraped my body
on rock and bark hoping to fly—cardinalis
cardinalis. Clad in leaves, reeking black,
familiar mud, I saw two rough lovers love,
I saw them love and move with terrible grace.
I swam and then I put on clothes and ran
through vacant lots. That half-chimney was still
standing, so was the houseful of stolen parts,
so was the fence where once a boy asked
to pay me just to drink my piss.
Where did I run, whose breathing you must
have heard, when I was thirteen or fourteen,
your own desire just beginning to speak openly
in my pulse? That random synapse leap
of the world caught me, too,
just as I broke into the open, just
as I busted through the trees.

Son, When I Hold You Tightly

to me on the divan in the meditative
time of day, next to me, your arms going

limp as you nod in and out of sleep,
having spent most of the day actively

in honest mockery of my own,
I cannot think of right words or cause

consonant, or why outside a male
cardinal flourishes in blank winter

grass, or why just now I reinvent
your nasal sound in this green plastic

cornet, unnerving, almost unalive,
and imagine your father's father's

drunken dance to that one repetitive
song of loud slurred whistles for five to ten

minutes out there in the old suburbs
of light and dazzle in the acrobatic,

predictable fifties, bright red and black-
throated, our unmistakable noise. I don't

remember our most unattended joy:
I remember tones and half notes

in the backyard. I sweat through daylight
to see the woman at the window,

staring out at what happened, tap, tapping
a knuckle or a pencil, or the sun's

position as read by the nature
of its glint. My mother's stare was neither

joy nor sorrow. Surely now it beckons
to me. She's wrapped in her apron of spaced-

out flowers in her woman's redemptive role
in the kitchen, blond hair, clear blue eyes

unmindful. She ghosts through the house.
I think of the pot roast steaming, then

of what things were *really* like, why this
woman with stark eyes doesn't swim into

my poems—her gentleness, her
particular depth and height as she

cocked her head and looked, her absolute
sway—she spoke me into focus, but

first she listened without separating
the wonderful from the probable.

Her memory is remarkable.
Her eyes reflect an unfamiliar

preening which became a part of the world.
She told me about anting, that process

by which a cardinal crushes an ant
and works it into her plumage, enchantment

for which I do not have a reason,
happiness for which I do not apologize.

I remember light and dark in my mother's eyes.

Anniversary of Wood

Anniversary of Wood

We have the corners to ourselves
black as that book bracing
the window, so how
do you understand marriage if not
through walking among separate
lives as if such intimacy were
possible? Light divulges itself
in the angles of your face.
You have just put on your clothes
and are making the bed, making up
the house and neighborhood and town
in a country of armchairs and divans
in a world of gray and purple smoke.
The grace with which you
walk across the room,
look back, walk again
into another room should have
told me something, should tell
me now. I have asked too
many questions, and none
will-lessly. Yet
you return, scholia, light of light.
And the years we have loved do.
Anguish, fatigue, unstable
balances, long and geometric silence
hardly recognize themselves at all.
The sun dazzles the complex carpentry
and fills your hair, caresses
your curves, your buttocks,
your lovely arrogant mouth.

Try

Put it all in,
Make use.
—*Ray Carver*

1

Twelve gongs of the Becker clock and I am back
to sleep where I imagine you dreaming of a former
lover, some groaning then those two ecstatic
cries, your hand anchored at your hip,
you on your back in the dark. Ridiculously
I find myself wondering if you're still happy
with me. You could be elsewhere, we might
have never met. Twelve gongs and I am back
unable to absorb my own absurd obsessions.
I swoon among details. Midnight pins
its one star simply by saying so, perceiving so.
I drift awkwardly lacking presence, away, not toward.

2

Yesterday we stopped at Talbott's and everything
was on. The fan blowing hot air, the second
hand of the Falstaff clock creeping,
the radio blaring, everything, but no Talbott.
We went on to the horse races and my
two friends who had wanted to introduce me
to him and his famous dirt-floor garage where he

held court and handed out free Falstaff were now
wondering if Talbott had "fallen out," a curious
military phrase labeling those who break formation
or fall out of line, the older man repeating the phrase
and also describing his own heart attack
two years back on the golf course; then for some reason
I heard in my head that Irish riddle which rings
and rings but seldom means anything to anybody:
What are three scarcities greater than any one immensity?
A scarcity of fancy talk.
In a wide field, a scarcity of crows.
A scarcity of friends around the drink.

                                Thank goodness . . .
the older guy telephoned and Talbott was okay.
He had just stepped out to buy a water pump.

My friends agreed they'd been foolish, worrying so much.
Then again, everything was on.
And why would Talbott want to leave his garage?
And what is verisimilitude that grown men
swoon in public out of love
with the thick cadence of what happens, what is man
that his own pulse sits in his ear with every word,
forcing absolute sway, sounding like everything,
shaking the sky, shaking the ground
like a striking of horses' hooves,
like a missile seeking heat halfway past the world.

What do I remember
        from what forgotten sounds
pooling below sea level where
        I lean and wash then
moor my face in logic
        of its forehead, bent ignoble
nose, mouth which wakes
        in fury, and empty ears?
Narcissus, we've lost a day.
        I snap the stem beneath
the basal leaves and smell
        six white petals from
the upper margin of its torn
        blouse, the mauve
center the size of a nipple.
        A car door slams. There is
an echo of feminine laughter,
        the voice unhinging, redoubled
in happiness and beauty,
        in its truth as it bounds
rebounding off the mountain wall.
        The way human sound can
fill a room like a perfect
        understanding of time.
The way the beloved
        speaks my name in sleep.

For My Wife, on Our Son's Third Birthday

This time he claims he's hitting a lion drive.
It takes two hours to get him inside, there
are two hundred rocks, there's a thick black pipe
running under the house which carries excrement,
there's a spider's web before the crawl space;
this time he's blowing a lion drive with soap
bubbles—up, up battering against wind but
lazily, its lion having bailed out early.
There is healing in the blood, there is sorrow
in the head. When I see us walk
in this self-made semicircle, when I think
of exuberance swinging somehow loose
from my son's wayward feet,
when I look without seeing at the bubble rising
to burst above the eave, without awareness
of its size, shape, color, duration,
when I remember for no reason or no apparent reason,
when my boy takes my hand and leads me
back down the buried drive and daylight dies
along my wrist, I who can't
link one thought to the other, I think, yes,
here comes our son, our soul,
higher than the practical pursuit of one thing,
floating like a bubble, hurled
like Lucretius's dart flying outward
beyond the bounds of the world.

Memory

All day long
My heart was in my knee,
But no hearing.
—*George Herbert*

Didn't I think of the clasp
or stirrup, that cartilage
beckoning the knee, surrounding it
and leading to cap and musculature, not
the physics but the metaphysics—
heat and sideways light—that fluid motion,
grace of my old man a little younger
than I am now; did I think of that
hatch and latch, sinking too;
did I think of that ache of pleasure
at wondering at myself age, not realizing
years later,
this persistence, dull all right,
radiates differently.
Didn't I think of something
during that casual golf swing
feeling a catch or twinge
minutes later, or remember that years ago
I could have tended a bruise like a fire,
lilted over pain—my lyric elegy,
that elegiac lyric—;
didn't I think of something almost accidental
like that easy swing
lifting over the trees—

if I could only retrace that movement in the body,
that circular plane
perfect and unrehearsed.
I put the ball on the tee.
That catch doesn't come until later.
I think of it as death,
self-inflicted, and I'm wrong.
I search with my fingers for that tendon,
that sharp inheritance, that impulse
under the skin prompting its hinge,
protuberant in cypresses
long in water, brought down
by force. Under cardboard, under
that bright bridge of concrete and steel,
under stars, under abutment and buttress,
arch and leaf brown as my old father's eyes,
under a traffic blowing by—
I dream of my son who bends
in the knees out of joy, William
out of the wild time unseen, sweet flower
of improvisation.

Swamp Candles

Force

He turns his shirt collar up and feels
the prickle of manhood on his neck as if
anywhere he goes the world will hold his image
but where his breathing goes, why it stings
the lining of his throat is hard to say
or name exactly so when he watches the woman
load her groceries then slam the station wagon
door then crawl into the driver's side,
turn the ignition and ease into the flow
of traffic, he follows the way nausea follows
fear, the way sugar and salt follow damp
magnolia sour on this night in the South
as he parks behind her and traps her
in her drive and quickly quickly makes her
disappear as if beneath an immaculate tablecloth
with only a torn sack and a few small cans
of corn toppling over and a stinging sensation
which they both recognize like a willow branch
across the legs; this way and over here
that smell of iron and taste of the St. Charles River,
those molecules which would stand up and scream
or cry, do anything, just make it stop—
is what makes his face lose control
after he smiles and says hello or good-bye
to you or someone like you or me which
he is and she is, neither born that way
but two driving east under colored lights
along rolling hills, she in the trunk,
he behind the wheel, past the country club
driving and driving into the second world.

Swimming Pool

We dropped rubber bricks to the bottom
and fought for yellow fins which flashed
through submarine blue to a glowing
opening where reasonable lawn chairs stared.
Now my gin sweats, the glass goes rubbery.
I sit on flagstone and watch my son
as he swims, dives, finds the surface
blinking, shaking his slick brown head.
My own breath rattles like an aluminum
ladder being extended in sleep. But
I can go back to rooms so clean and
stark only the cinder block listens,
to the public institution where I lived
when swimming meant water was what
you didn't know and ignorance gave
knowledge unintended grace. My son
is diving now. He screams for me
to look. Sometimes we are too much
the same backward dive arcing and
extending, every breathing place looking
out of its socket. But always I am
awakened by his presence. He rises
to the surface. I stand too
and clap too hard and long
without meaning to. He climbs
the ladder, looks up, glowers, shakes
me off like seaweed. I let go.
If not, my son knows enough to let

me go, to bring a knife if need be
and to swim to the sky like a merman.
If I were to wave about and struggle
or tug on his ankles like a meadow
under the sea, he would cut loose
like I taught him and swim back through
his shadow and rise with hair clinging close
to his scalp but finned on top.

Adam's Birthday

The boy whose father made him make
him a pot of coffee before he could
leave the house has a birthday today.
His ectomorphic brow shades his six-year-
old eyes of chronic concern, which are
ordinary enough light blue. We
are always walking into three leaves
and an electric saw drowning out
the voice faring forward. I want
to swim, says Adam. Okay, there's the water.
So he cannonballs, water explodes
in warm air. I want to make books not poems.
But first individual grunts and groans,
words and glue like mouth-
matter, then sentences and
paragraphs, the insinuation of
ideas, endless talk which puts
off death almost successfully.
Summer turns into fall, the
flagstone darkens then shimmers in
daylight like invisible stars,
Adam grows up, goes off, his
father goes mumbling into whatever
like his namesake who knew better
than to go alone. No doubt
the swimming pool still wavers
unnatural blue in the sclera
of seasonal sun. But the walking

away which was like the walking
toward stiffens in anguish
because water will abandon,
the green stars wheel discretely
like a thousand separations.

The Happy Story

My father's eyelids drooped as he
would tell it, how he wandered
in the wrong apartment, touched a
woman, not his wife, sleeping with a man.
He sat down on the bed and touched her
shoulder more tenderly than anything
he loved knowing even then somehow
that he would have to leave
the same way he came past the
silk lampshade, across the oak floor
of rivers of feeling for another
man's wife, that he would need
to withdraw his hands which had always
been small, that he would be telling
this story to his sons even after
his life was over, that this moment
of happiness would not live in him
but in his issue . . . strange word,
that, and nobody woke, not even
the dog and cat of the human voice
chasing animal desire, and the porch
stayed dark and swayed in its shadow
like a drunk fishing for keys
and stars stayed lit like boys
who are buddies yelling from their Dodge,
and we and mine are asleep and the house
cooks as it ticks in Enid, Oklahoma,
where we rent two rooms and a kitchen
and laughter spills like milk-shine.
A train passes, glasses creak,
a sweet harmonic takes itself away.

To My Father in Heaven

"There you are you son of a bitch,"
    I said waking in ignorance, raising
        my fists, then standing suddenly

asking, "What? . . ." I heard
    myself say, "William," meaning
        son of my heart, father

of my dreaming, father of fathers,
    who murdered yourself in your own bed
        in your trailer house.

And wind harps as it nudges the wires
    so that there's warping
        in the already strange

message which drifts just short
    of a desire to speak,
        making the phone ring

in its phoniness on the distressed
    pine table. I think the message
        is nonessential since every grief

is one and the same. I think that because
    to be responsible for one's words
        means to suspect them.

Still I cannot dream you speaking.
    There in the doorway you leaned and evaporated.
      You roll in blackness on the waves of sleep.

       *

There were many, there are few of you—
    all patrons of the dark,
      musty but with sweet hops and barley smell,

Angie tending bar, and Mr. Lee,
    whose long fingernails bit the flesh
      counting out yellow stacks

of tens and twenties, saying something unimportant
    to a woman bent to sip her beer,
      and now you're screaming, you're yelling again

in some private blur, having imagined
    that Lee welched on a bet.
      I don't know why the three ball

hangs on the corner pocket,
    but it does when the sound comes out,
      and Lee bids you adieu,

he bids you get the fuck out.
    The clacking of pinball returns,
      so does the ringing of bells

and faces sparkle in glass, and dominoes
    find their tables and the flies
        as you, my father,

turn from one stage to another,
    and walk out the door.
        The sky pulls you up,

the aluminum pie plate tied to a stick
    shakes a little. It shimmers
        in the iris of the rabbit

who waits until night and nibbles
    on the lettuce and lightly
        dances and sings the song that he

fooled you, everything too large
    with dried blood sprinkled
        on the ground, baked to flakes as big

as kosher salt, bleached with information
    which says this is you, your stink
        under heaven, your scent upon the earth.

*

There were many, now there are few.
    There's a thick white pillow
        where your head comes down—

There's oil and dirt flecks
        and a wash of human flesh on silk.
                Sweat and salt only sweet like meat

in bone. And the last thing you hold
        is a yellow rose because
                of some story that somebody told.

That's the truth. That's that.
        From where they put you back
                they laid you out.

I remember from here in the future
        in Little Rock in the backyard
                of my house on a hill.

Isn't this the wagging privet branch
        like a single strand of hair,
                near evening, not much stir

but only a robin's miniature swoop
        from telephone wire to
                pine. Then in purple dusk

you see his flight, you can feel it
        in tones and lines and curves.
                The terror of being taken,

particle and wave extrude,
        the surface tension of water
                anticipates nothing—

we go and we don't make sense,
     we stay and we recognize what
          in us we hate, but we say

I want to love, I am
     no longer part of this,
          I am so alone that my reach

extends to my fingertips.
     If a current pulls and pulls—
          it pulled you best—deep

and late a cold assuming pressure.
     What if the pressure isn't pain
          but impatience—not to understand

but to live without knowledge
     of death, not to resolve but to live
          too quickly? How does it happen

that pain becomes impatient
     to walk out in the leaves? I
          think I know and that is because I fear

when I speak that my own voice comes back
     and I will not survive, like you.
          What is all this talk, what

is it to need so much, is
     it power, only deep and shallow
          with a silvering echo

like light around a shovel and a hoe?
  I smell a damp upturned dirt—it
    goes deep in the nostril but not enough.

That would be too easy to say.
  A sweet salt liquefies
    the words before they sour,

the grief they hurry
  is old, unsupernatural, impossible
    to swallow.

Real Time

Real Time

When the thought of a thought
lives itself and then its
other lives, and your mother
    and I read you a quick story,
        a mystery chosen by you

from your library at school,
and time calls spinning still
in its clock, the one we
    gave as we took, took not
        from my family but your

mother's, her mother's
white rocking still so that
sleep is the same, when time
    does this—calls,
        calls you back—

know that he or she
is not a thief asleep by
the river—nor one already
    carried far and away, all
        those waves of darkness

hardened over years. We have
accused knowledge but knowing
nothing has kept us
  from our fear and that,
      that is our calling

  and what we have not thought
all these years.

Suburb of Light and Dazzle

June comes on flirtingly like a high soprano
feminine laugh in the basement followed by two

voices, male and female mumbling, then sudden
quiet, all but something crazed and wooden

like a mop handle knocking up in the trees
but it's down below with heat you can't hear.

They agree to meet again at night where bats
strike liquid stars in the face with their wings.

Or they flutter and roam like Virgil's poor
unburied dead. Or swarm with birds to build

a wall in the sky, not knowing what they are doing,
having been touched by a great love and not knowing it.

Paint cans topple and the air gets close,
down and down in the basement, where weight

shifts in its desire. What sends the mind away?
What creates beauty is the light of justice

in the attention, said Simone Weil, from behind
her candle of heat and love on her kitchen

table in the beginning of the month of June,
when flagstone burns the feet but night chills.

The Hope of Mississippi

Lady Luck. Just over the river and east
through Tunica. You go with coupons
and a fixed amount, no credit cards
or checks but a realization with Alphonse
Carr that the quicker it goes the longer it lasts.
And you would call her a shooter, the gray
woman who shakes her fist then throws numbers—
who talks awhile with others
while the others talk
because they'll never see her or she
them again unless the numbers combine
just so. How else do I know that goldenrod
on the drive home sweeps
nothing but blank blue?
How else do I broom up
an answer for my son
at bedtime after I've read him
Icarus? His question: How would you rescue me?
My answer: I'd fly up and get you.
But what if you couldn't do that
either? I'd wear a beanie
to make you laugh. Then
he puts his head on the pillow,
swamp candles all along the top
and bottom land, ryegrass smell
of stars in the air.

Slug Caterpillar

Yellow stinging hair extending, mostly
brown with some green markings and silver
like the inside of a mouse's ear,
short thoracic legs, a whole team
of Minnie Minosas hogging home plate—
it isn't until now, my mother visiting,
that I learn about myelodystlastia,
as we sit drinking coffee at the kitchen
table and watch the rain overtake
the garden. We open the window
to smell it, drops like gooseflesh.
She who cannot remember the word for trampoline,
confuses it with tambourine, sticks
on the term for her sister's illness,
the description of her walker, four-
pronged, and her bent shuffling walk.
Wind picks up and day grows grayer.
Maybe the slurring speech of my
mother makes a ladder to the sky,
or maybe rain comes in waves
and families watch and listen
and make precise categories for
lightning and phases of the moon.
It is raining and it's going to rain.
We watch it darken and deepen and rain.

Wild Walking: After the Gulf War

1

When they drove to the crappie lake on those
humid, four o'clock mornings, lights coming on
in Woolworth's, someone pulling out
of Crescent Donuts in a Chevrolet mottled rust,
slowly, like a shorebird legend has doesn't exist,
his father and he talked; but he can't remember
what about, only that the car's interior
seems now, to him, lit. He heard the car door
slam, and the trunk, then again, that noise
floating away from them in low, chrome-colored
mist to where sky wrapped its tightness with no
purpose or systematic reasoning different
from the boy's as he pulled his shoes off
before bedtime the night before, even less,
less reasoning or purpose over water so flat
and far-reaching all the way across *what is,*
just then crowning, the top of its head almost
                                    appearing.
That was Lake Tenkiller, Cherokee County, Oklahoma,
just as the sun was coming up. I
do not see the child's body bending to his
father, leaning close to his ear so that speaking
makes a noise again now.

2

I drift in time and space to my son's metal monkey bars
and how I submerge, come evening, the four legs
in concrete about a foot deep with help from
my wife. Of course we argue. Our neighbor appears
        behind
her screen and says, "They like to fight at night," not
        referring
to us as we think at first but to the American
air-raid on Baghdad. She insists that our project will
        wobble
no matter what when the kid goes hand over hand
with his full weight.
                              Next morning
I prime with oil base a wood trellis
to make it last at least as long as the climbing
rose it supports and there I make a drip appear
on the otherwise shining strip. Israel
tapes her windows, caulks her doors
and keyholes and cracks; Iraq sleeps
obsessively amid F-14s and Phantom flak.
I watch by satellite the effect of Scud missiles.
Scud meaning to drift briskly as though over water,
to be thrown like a stone beyond influence.

3

That poor bastard, who is he paraded out
on Iraqi news as a prisoner of war, and made
to read prepared speech, poor son of a bitch
with leaking left eye and busted lip?
What is he thinking, does he remember
a rusted bolt he might have kicked up while
scuffing a bank somewhere, the one he
might have tied to nylon and cast because of its weight
which took it all the way down, took his
minnow hooked in the side near the tail?
Last night I slept as he bailed out and opened
his chute to the desert in the middle of the day
sun-blind and alive on a dog-head shape of land.

4

Dhahran, Riyadh, Batman, Bahrain, Incirlik—
names on a map in this map of names—I remember
learning about the Tigris and Euphrates from my hollow
desk in grade school, bolted to the floor, my mind
wandering in its vapor like a drunken fisherman.
I watch the television shapes of war,
cross-haired squares and rectangles.
A crumbling building ripples like a crappie pond.
Imagine the sky overcast, sunshine like
spoonbait drawn through water barely lucent,
wobbling above hook and silt murk. In Tel Aviv
a window hangs at an angle dangling in its casement
four stories up pooling in this January night, *jungle
hour*, Lowell called it, moonless, dead sober,
granting absolutely nothing.

5

Free-fallen, unhinged, choiceless, I land at home
in the Middle South in daylight. I remember falling
and drifting from the holy city, which is
always. Here fields are soy and wheat and pecan orchards,
some corn. There's the old cotton gin and church with
    square
steeple rising out of one corner, the bald cypresses
in the oxbow lake hollow enough for a child.
Down the road a cemetery, a shotgun
house on stilts, a commissary with bars on windows
next to the mansion "Marlsgate," where credit accounts
    were
kept in walnut until harvest. The names disappear,
the years float forward, a house floats down Highway 30
on eighteen wheels toward the fog-bottom delta.
                    How much is gone?

6

I remember John Hemphill. "I built that," said
John Hemphill. He placed the iron supporting jacks
under the corner joist and raised the roof.
I see the new neighbor's silver motorcar
climbing our whore of a hill like a glint
in the finish which is nostalgia. Tell me again
how to fix the ceiling, hand me the crowbar,
and hammer, and nails. I had only wanted to borrow
the wooden hammer, hand-turned, tapered at the neck.
It hangs in John Hemphill's shed now, the eyelets
and marls bear his salt. I can almost remember
the color and appearance of his skin, the inner surface
of the hand between the wrist and the base of the fingers.

7

            If there's meaning
there must be validity in it. What was
           time immemorial
is actually a string of moments. It takes on
importance in the sentence, it floats
like a dog's leg while he sleeps on his back,
his yellow fur catches a little breeze,
his long white fur stands on his belly
like a white carnation, like mood music:
I once had no mercy, now I have mercy.
What does it mean to say that war's inevitable?
If there's meaning it must be well-founded,
must include suspense yet cut off possibility.

8

"All I heard was a whistle and a wham, wham, wham,"
said America's first infantryman with a Purple Heart,
"I feel kind of special now." In twenty-four hours
Iraqi ground troops invade Saudi Arabia with armored
    tanks.
The image onscreen portends a past war; a perfect
pitch of words cut off from meaning; from first,
second, or third intention; from all efforts
toward this or that, this which is from need and desire,
that which is increasing or causing to increase—
come down, fly down, say what you are, what
are you not? Are you the snipe skimming the Oklahoma
    water?
Do I hold a bag for you? Do I smell the burlap dust
and taste your laughter? All I hear is a whistle
or a whisper up close in the ear like a child's voice
calling me. All I see are the little wires at eye level.

9

Neruda said it best: The blood of children runs
in the streets like the blood of children.
                            More or less exactly
east-northeast the constellation Boötes appears
over the Iraqi man weeping over his fallen potatoes.
Or is it that he's reminded of his daughter's
full face by all those eyes, as she gazed
one day at a ladybug climbing over her sleeve
and down her forearm and wrist?
She looked at her father and said,
"I like its wild walking."
Now her father gets up and stumbles
without her, wildly walking so that
when a star streaks someone is dying.

10

Across Tenkiller the willows are bright orange.
The B-52 returns by way of the old routes,
the land drops off behind it. Our war's over already,
we whistle into air, and the lake is dark
with mist and a fog settles, not that we coast
but think so thoughtlessly, not that we have
no reach but put our hands on nothing, not
that we have no motive but have no will
impelled by love. In the beginning was the word
and darkness wiped its sleeve across its mouth.
At the start were two children. Then language.
Then love which passeth understanding.
But that was morning and evening of the first day.

THE IOWA POETRY PRIZE WINNERS

1987

Elton Glaser, *Tropical Depressions*

Michael Pettit, *Cardinal Points*

1988

Bill Knott, *Outremer*

Mary Ruefle, *The Adamant*

1989

Conrad Hilberry, *Sorting the Smoke*

Terese Svoboda, *Laughing Africa*

1993

Tom Andrews, *The Hemophiliac's Motorcycle*

Michael Heffernan, *Love's Answer*

John Wood, *In Primary Light*

1994

James McKean, *Tree of Heaven*

Bin Ramke, *Massacre of the Innocents*

Ed Roberson, *Voices Cast Out to Talk Us In*

1995

Ralph Burns, *Swamp Candles*

Maureen Seaton, *Furious Cooking*

THE EDWIN FORD PIPER POETRY AWARD WINNERS

1990

Philip Dacey, *Night Shift at the Crucifix Factory*

Lynda Hull, *Star Ledger*

1991

Greg Pape, *Sunflower Facing the Sun*

Walter Pavlich, *Running near the End of the World*

1992

Lola Haskins, *Hunger*

Katherine Soniat, *A Shared Life*